DEDICATION

For my one true love, Jeff Hart.

3-Steps to Hire Your Ideal Divorce Attorney

Nichole Wilde Hart

CONTENTS

ACKNOWLEDGMENTS

I owe the totality of who I am to the influence of many wonderful people that I have had the pleasure and opportunity to work with throughout my life. This book was made possible thanks to Mr. Robert Von Dohlen, for whom I have worked and collaborated with to build a robust, thriving and surprisingly, low-drama, divorce practice. I also have deep and abiding gratitude for my long-time mentor, Lee Milteer, who has held my feet to the fire continuously for several years.

Chapter 1

Do I Have to Hire an Attorney to Help Me with My Divorce?

You might be surprised to learn that the answer is, no, you do not have to have an attorney help you with your divorce. Most counties in the USA have family law facilitators that can guide you to the documents that you need to complete and file with your county's court clerk to get the divorce process started. If you have been married for a short time, you have no children with your spouse and you do not have significant community and/or separate assets or a business to divide, filing the paperwork yourself is a practical and affordable option. Each individual State has laws regarding how long a divorce takes. I recommend that you search Google for your State's "Law Help" resource website to learn more about how the process works in your State.

Let me share with you a few stories that illustrate

why I believe it is a bad idea to go through a divorce without the representation of a wonderful attorney.

Tom and Beth divorced quickly in 2018. They were both smart and absolutely hated the thought of giving one penny to attorneys in their asset division. Beth happily signed the papers that Tom put together and the judge signed off on their uncontested divorce. The uncontested divorce where he saddled himself with 10 years of continued close relationship with a woman he wanted to be divorced from, because of his "reasonable" effort to be good to Beth. The deal was, after a certain life event the community home was to be sold and divided, however he neglected to define the terms explicitly and accurately and when he came shopping for an attorney to help him untangle his mess five years later, he was regretful. He wished he HAD hired an attorney at the beginning because that would have cost him 1/3 of what he was about to invest in fixing his mistake, finally freeing himself from what seemed like extra painful, post-divorce bondage to Beth.

A few of you might be asking, why did the judge sign off on an order that was obviously not thorough or fair? Due to the overwhelming case load, more than 3,000 new cases each month, the judges in Harris County, Texas, have about 3 minutes to focus their attention on your case. It's just unreasonable to even expect that they would catch your mistakes and save you from yourself. That's not what they are there for. That's what your ideal divorce attorney is there for!

Carla had been so hopeful when Juan had said he had signed the waiver of service for their divorce. She felt so relieved that they were not going to be shelling out thousands of dollars each just to divide their businesses. They had been married 25 years; had built everything together: his trucking company and her salon empire. This was going to work out just fine. And then. She had become frustrated waiting for him to get the paperwork back to her so she could file it and soon realized her mistake when she was met by a process server in her driveway. They were still living together. He was suing her for divorce, accusing her of adultery, and asking for everything including full custody of their two minor children.

We often, sadly, lie to ourselves. We lie about the partner that we know, even when we know all too well their behavior and tactics. Looking back, Carla knew that any attempt to work on a collaborative divorce with Juan was going to be impossible. They had been married and created two businesses, fighting tooth and nail the entire time. How the heck would they collaborate in divorce when they couldn't collaborate in life? She wished she had saved herself from the trauma and had the emotional advantage of being the one who filed first. She regrets not consulting an attorney before she asked her husband for a divorce.

Many, many times in life we find that we are time, money, and peace of mind ahead to hire a professional to help us solve our problems. I am a firm believer that this is especially true in the case of divorce. Hiring the right attorney for you is imperative. Dissolving your marriage is a big deal, and you need and deserve a trusted legal advisor by your side throughout the process. Divorce is hard enough! Make your life exponentially easier by hiring an attorney who will work with you in a way that is professional, filled with communication and get the job done as quickly as possible so your family can step out into its "New Normal" with peace and ease.

The aim of this book is to guide you in shopping, vetting, interviewing, choosing and hiring not just any attorney. That's easy. Grab your credit card and enter a Google search. Hire the first person you call. The aim of this book is to help you hire your IDEAL attorney.

Divorce is never ideal, however, when you do need a divorce, you want your ideal divorce attorney by your side. Let this book be your guide. Onward, toward your best life!

Chapter 2

The Power of Simplicity

In an age of information overload, the divorce process can seem like a daunting maze. The emotional, financial, and logistical challenges accompanying such a decision often leave individuals feeling overwhelmed and indecisive. One of the most critical choices to make, often ironically paralleling the difficulty of the decision to divorce itself, is selecting the right attorney to represent your interests. When standing at this crossroads, complexity is not your ally. Instead, simplicity is the compass you need. That's where the '3-Steps to Hiring Your Ideal Divorce Attorney.'

Why Simplicity Matters

In the words of Leonardo da Vinci, "Simplicity is the ultimate sophistication." Simplicity isn't about cutting corners or compromising quality; it's about stripping away the unnecessary to reveal the essence. This is particularly crucial when it comes to legal matters where the stakes are high, such as divorce.

The divorce process is riddled with decisions that can have long-lasting effects on your financial well-being, emotional health, and family dynamics. With so much at stake, the last thing you need is additional confusion or complications. Simplifying the attorney selection process can give you the clarity to decide confidently, knowing you've adhered to a well-thought-out method.

Simplicity vs. Complexity in the World of Divorce Attorneys

The realm of divorce attorneys is vast and diverse. Some lawyers dabble in various areas of law, from criminal defense to real estate, only touching family law now and then. Others might have flashy advertisements on billboards or local TV channels, promising swift victories without adequately understanding your unique situation.

Complexity thrives in this environment. Many potential clients find themselves entangled in lengthy consultations, buried under legal jargon, or worse, ensnared in hidden fee structures. These intricate paths can lead to delayed decisions, higher costs, and, at times, the unfortunate choice of an ill-suited attorney. In contrast, a direct, simple approach circumvents these pitfalls, leading you more swiftly and surely to the right professional fit.

A Beacon in the Fog

The "Direct Approach" is more than just a strategy; it's a philosophy. It acknowledges that you, the client, have specific needs, desires, and boundaries that are non-negotiable. By advocating for a direct interaction with potential attorneys, you cut through the generic sales pitches and get to the heart of what matters: Can this attorney represent me effectively? Do our values align? Can I trust this person to navigate me through one of the most challenging periods of my life?

The direct approach doesn't waste time on maybes. It's about clear 'yes' or 'no' answers, making your journey to finding the right attorney shorter and more precise.

Chapter 3

Breaking Down the Three Steps

Before you can find the perfect attorney, you must first understand what you're looking for. This step pushes you to introspect, to clearly delineate what you want out of the divorce process. Whether it's retaining custody of your children, safeguarding specific assets, or ensuring a smooth, amicable split, knowing your goals upfront will guide your attorney search. It also involves setting boundaries concerning communication, fees, and the attorney's approach, ensuring there are no unpleasant surprises down the line.

It's crucial to dive deeper into the nuances of this introspection and goal-setting process. This foundational step is not just about listing your desires but about a thorough self-assessment and understanding of the legal landscape you're about to navigate. Here are some expanded thoughts on this:

Self-Assessment and Clarity of Goals

Understanding Your Priorities: Begin by identifying what is most important to you in the divorce. Is it the well-being of your children, the equitable division of assets, or perhaps maintaining a cordial relationship with your ex-spouse for the sake of family harmony? Prioritizing these aspects will help you communicate your needs more effectively to your attorney.

Long-Term Vision: Consider not just the immediate outcomes of the divorce, but also the long-term implications. How will your decisions affect your life and those of your children in the years to come? This might include considerations around relocation: where will you live? Career changes; Will you need to change jobs to be able to afford life solo? and changes in your lifestyle.

Boundaries: It's important to set clear boundaries with your attorney regarding what you are and aren't willing to compromise on. This can include your bottom line in negotiations, your privacy, and the extent to which you want to be involved in every decision.

Expectations: Clear communication about your expectations and understanding the realistic outcomes of your case can help in setting a collaborative tone with your attorney. This includes being open to receiving advice that might not always align with your initial wishes but is in your best interest legally and personally.

Emotional Support and Guidance

While your attorney's primary role is to provide legal representation, the emotional toll of divorce cannot be underestimated. Consider the level of emotional support and guidance you might need from your attorney. Some clients may prefer a more detached, strictly professional relationship, while others might seek an attorney who provides emotional reassurance and support through the process.

By taking the time to introspect and clearly define

what you're looking for in a divorce attorney, you're more likely to find someone who not only meets your legal needs but also aligns with your personal values and goals for the future. This preparatory step is essential in navigating the divorce process with more confidence and a sense of control over the outcomes.

Directly Engage & Qualify Potential Candidates:

Instead of passively accepting referrals or going with the first name on a Google search list, this step is about proactive engagement. It involves direct discussions, pointed questions, and gauging the attorney's reactions to understand their expertise and ethos. The objective is to sift through the masses and shortlist only those professionals who align with your needs and values. As you search through the listings on your favorite search engine, compile a list of firms that you will reach out to. Set aside a block of time to just call and talk to law firms about your case. Take careful notes.

Commit & Collaborate for Victory:

Once you've found a potential fit, this step focuses on setting the stage for a successful partnership. It's not just about hiring the attorney but also about ensuring you both are on the same page. Regular communication, feedback loops, and being clear about expectations are paramount. After all, the attorney-client relationship is a two-way street.

Knowledge is Power

'3-Steps to Hire Your Ideal Divorce Attorney' is more than just a process; it's an empowerment tool. It recognizes the emotional toll of divorce and offers a streamlined approach to one of its most critical components: selecting your legal representation. By embracing simplicity and a direct method, you're not only ensuring a smoother legal process but also taking a significant stride towards healing and starting a new chapter with confidence.

Chapter 4

The Crucial Decision

In the world of geology, tectonic plates, unseen and colossal, shift beneath the earth's surface. Their movements, subtle yet profound, can lead to monumental changes, even earthquakes. Similarly, beneath the tumultuous surface of human relationships, decisions are made that dictate the course of life. One such decision, akin to the shifting of those great plates, is the choice of a divorce attorney.

It was in the quiet study of a vintage home, its walls lined with books that bore witness to countless legal battles, that I first met Attorney Jameson. His office was filled with the scent of old leather and subdued light filtered through heavy drapes. On his mahogany desk lay a single photograph, a little girl with bouncing curls - his daughter. This image, emblematic of countless such stories, serves as a compass for Jameson in navigating the turbulent waters of divorce litigation. As he succinctly put it, "The stakes are real; the outcomes, life-altering."

Attorney Jameson's metaphorical comparison between the complexities of geology and the intricacy of human emotion is apt. Both fields require a delicate balance of knowledge, intuition, and an understanding of forces far larger than oneself.

The professional you choose to represent you in a divorce is the intermediary between these tectonic forces, attempting to find equilibrium amid the chaos.

For many, a divorce is not just the dissolution of a legal bond but a dismantling of shared dreams, aspirations, and years of shared history. Much like a geologist studying the layers of the earth, an attorney must sift through these layers of shared experiences, assets, grievances, and hopes to arrive at a resolution. The sensitivity, skill, and expertise of this professional can significantly influence the outcome, just as the finesse of a geologist can determine the interpretation of an intricate rock formation.

But why, one might ask, is the choice of an attorney so pivotal? Can't any trained legal professional guide one through the labyrinth of legal procedures?

To answer that, consider the Delaware Water Gap, a marvel of geology where the Delaware River cuts through a large ridge of the Appalachian Mountains. This natural wonder didn't form overnight. It's the result of years of persistent erosion, water working against rock. A divorce, in many cases, is the culmination of years of erosion – of trust, of love, of shared goals. Just as each section of the Delaware Water Gap tells a unique story of geological history, every divorce has its unique narrative.

The attorney you choose is entrusted with the task of understanding your narrative, the years of erosion, the moments of significance, and the layers of complexities. They become the voice of your story in the courtroom. A mismatch between the narrative and its narrator can lead to misinterpretations, miscalculations, and in the realm of divorce – grave injustices.

Moreover, beyond the courtroom, the chosen attorney plays a pivotal role in guiding one through the emotional whirlwind that divorce often brings. Their approach, demeanor, and even their own experiences with the judicial system and its emotional toll can influence one's journey from a life shared to a life independent.

The tremors of a divorce, much like those caused by shifting tectonic plates, have aftershocks. These reverberations, be it in the form of custody battles, alimony disputes, or emotional distress, can linger for years, even a lifetime. Hence, the importance of that crucial decision - the choice of attorney - cannot be overstated. The right attorney can stabilize the ground beneath one's feet, making the tremors manageable, even navigable. The wrong choice, however, can amplify the aftershocks, leaving lasting scars on the emotional and financial landscape of one's life.

In the world of shifting terrains, be it the complexities of the earth's crust or the intricate web of human relationships, navigators like geologists and attorneys become indispensable. Their expertise, approach, and the tools they employ can make all the difference.

For those standing on the precipice of such a significant life decision, understanding the gravity of the choice before them is paramount.

In the dim light of Attorney Jameson's study, as we concluded our conversation, he pointed once again to the photograph of his daughter. "This is my compass," he said softly. For those on the brink of divorce, the right attorney becomes not just a legal representative but also a compass, guiding them through the uncharted terrains of heartbreak, hope, and renewal.

The weight of that choice, and its potential consequences, are as profound and far-reaching as the movements of the very earth beneath our feet.

Chapter 5

Defining The Terrain

In the rugged landscapes of the American West, the vast terrains are marked by shifts and rifts, each crevice and plateau telling a story millions of years in the making. To the untrained eye, these landscapes may appear static, unchanging; yet, to a geologist every nuance, from the grandest canyon to the smallest pebble, speaks of dynamic processes at play.

Similarly, the landscape of human relationships is marked by its own shifts and rifts, especially at the precipice of a decision as monumental as divorce. Just as a geologist begins their exploration with a clear understanding of what they're seeking—be it a particular mineral deposit or evidence of a prehistoric event—those embarking on the path of divorce must first clearly delineate their goals and non-negotiables. This is the essential bedrock upon which the rest of the process will unfold.

Realizing the Stakes

Understanding the stakes in a divorce is akin to understanding the geological significance of a landscape. At first glance, one might see a divided household, shared assets, and joint bank accounts. But delving deeper, much like an earth scientist would with his chisel and magnifying glass, reveals layers of complexities: the emotional well-being of children, long-term financial implications, and the profound reshaping of individual futures.

Assets: In the economic terrain of a marriage, assets are like mineral deposits. They represent accumulations over time—be it in the form of property, investments, or simple savings. To some, these assets represent security, to others, memories, and for many, they are a combination of both. Splitting these assets is seldom a straightforward task. It requires understanding not just their monetary value, but also their emotional and symbolic significance. Just as a geologist would painstakingly map out an area before any excavation, a divorcing individual must take stock of shared assets, deciding which ones are most valuable, not just in monetary terms, but in the grander schema of their life's landscape.

Child Custody: If assets are the mineral deposits, then children are the life-giving rivers that flow through the marital landscape. The question of their custody is perhaps the most emotionally charged aspect of any divorce. Here, the stakes transcend the immediate parties involved, influencing young, impressionable lives. The decisions made will shape their psychological terrain, their sense of stability, and their future relationships. Ensuring their well-being requires a meticulous understanding of their needs, emotional and physical, and a commitment to prioritizing them above all else.

Alimony/ Spousal Support: The concept of alimony, much like the erosion processes in geology, speaks to the wear and tear of time. It's a recognition that in the shared journey of marriage, sacrifices were made, opportunities were foregone, and roles were assumed that might have economic implications post-divorce. Determining alimony is not just about financial support; it reflects the past. It's an attempt to balance the scales, to ensure that the erosion of time doesn't leave one party to the dissolved partnership in an economic desert while the other thrives.

Your Future: Beyond the tangible and immediate, lies the vast horizon of the future—much like the expansive skies that stretch above our geological formations. This future, once visualized together, now requires reimagining. Where will you live? What will your financial health look like? How will you rebuild emotionally? The answers to these questions are the North Stars guiding the divorce process, ensuring that the decisions made align with the future you envision.

In the end, much like the Earth's terrains that bear silent testimony to the relentless march of geological time, the landscape of a divorcing individual's life will bear the marks of this profound transition. But with clarity, understanding the stakes, and guided by well-defined goals, this reshaped terrain can be one of resilience, renewal, and hope.

Those navigating divorce can find meaning,

strength, and a clear path forward by meticulously defining their goals and understanding the profound stakes at play. The terrain might be rugged, the path arduous, but with clarity as their compass, they can navigate towards a horizon of hope and new beginnings.

Navigating the Terrain

Amidst the vast plains of the American Midwest, where the horizon stretches endlessly in every direction, there lies a patchwork of farmlands, rivers, and settlements. Each plot, each meander, each hamlet tells its own tale—of dreams sown, of legacies nurtured, of futures envisioned. Imagine yourself with the uncanny ability to perceive profound stories in landscapes; you would discern a tapestry of life and time in this tableau. Similarly, in the sprawling plains of human relationships, when the horizon of marriage is disrupted by the looming shadow of divorce, the stakes are manifold, each with its own intricate narrative: assets, alimony, child custody, and the undulating path to a reshaped future.

The Bedrock of Shared Endeavors

Assets, in the landscape of marriage, are akin to the fertile tracts in the heartland. They represent the labor of seasons, the investments of time, and the aspirations of a shared future. Be it the first home bought with combined savings, the artwork acquired during a memorable trip, or the joint venture birthed from mutual dreams, these assets are not mere economic entities. They are milestones, markers of shared experiences and intertwined dreams.

When the specter of divorce looms, these assets become contested terrains. To divvy them up requires not just an understanding of their monetary value, but also a deep appreciation of their emotional and historical significance. It's like partitioning a plot of ancestral land: the worth isn't just in the soil, but in the memories that saturate it. In navigating this terrain, one must tread with both fairness and sensitivity, ensuring that in the division, the essence of bygone days isn't lost or undervalued.

The Erosion of Time

Water, as it courses through landscapes, gradually carves valleys, shapes coastlines, and redefines terrains. Over time, the continuous flow reshapes even the most formidable mountains, turning them into gentle hills. Marriage, with its ebb and flow of roles, responsibilities, and sacrifices, similarly wears down individual paths, reshaping personal trajectories. Alimony/ Spousal Support emerges from this understanding, recognizing that the flow of time and the compromises made in a relationship often leave indelible marks.

Determining alimony isn't merely an economic exercise. It's an endeavor to acknowledge sacrifices, to respect choices made for the greater good of the union, and to ensure that as two lives diverge, they do so with a semblance of balance. Like ensuring that a river, after carving a valley, continues to nourish it, alimony seeks to prevent economic desolation after the erosion of time.

Nurturing the Future Groves

If one were to walk the forests of the Pacific Northwest, they'd meet ancient groves—trees that have stood for centuries, bearing witness to time's march. In the marital ecosystem, children are akin to these ancient groves. They are the legacies, the continuities, the life forces that bridge past and future. Their well-being, in the context of divorce, becomes a terrain both delicate and paramount.

The stakes transcend mere logistical considerations. Where they will live, which school they'll attend, which holidays they'll spend with whom—these are important, yes. But more profound are the emotional terrains: ensuring stability, maintaining bonds, preserving a sense of belonging. Like forest conservators ensuring the well-being of ancient groves, parents, and legal mediators must prioritize the holistic well-being of children, preserving their emotional ecosystems even as familial landscapes shift.

The Future: Charting New Horizons

As one traverses the Rocky Mountains, each ascent culminates in a vantage point, revealing horizons previously unseen. Divorce, though punctuated by the pain of separation, also offers a vantage point—a chance to view horizons of individual futures, to chart paths previously unimagined.

Reimagining life post-divorce is both daunting and liberating. Financially, emotionally, and socially, new terrains await. Will there be a move to a new city? A career pivot? New relationships? Like a mountaineer plotting the next expedition, this stage requires preparation, courage, and a vision. It's an opportunity to sculpt the landscape of one's life, informed by the past but not bound by it.

The landscape of divorce is a tapestry of stakes and stories. Assets, alimony, child custody, and the journey towards a new future form its contours.

Navigating this landscape demands both pragmatism and sensitivity, a balance of head and heart. While the path might be strewn with challenges, with the right compass—of clarity, understanding, and empathy— and a great legal guide one can traverse it with dignity, hope, and resilience.

The Business of Heartbreak

In the annals of decision-making, few choices can be as profoundly personal as those tied to heartstrings, especially when those strings begin to unravel. Divorce, a terrain of emotional upheaval, is punctuated with choices that demand clarity amidst chaos. One of the most critical decisions during this tumultuous phase is the choice of a divorce attorney. While the impulse might be to let emotions lead, there's wisdom in approaching this choice much like a strategic business decision. Here's why:

Objectivity Amidst Subjectivity

In the corporate world, decisions—be it hiring, investments, or partnerships—are rarely made on emotion alone. Emotions, while valuable, can cloud judgment, leading to choices that might feel right momentarily but have long-term repercussions. Similarly, the choice of a divorce attorney, if driven by emotional impulses, can lead to regrettable outcomes.

An attorney is, essentially, your representative in this transitional phase. A mismatch between your expectations and their approach can lead to unnecessary friction, prolonging an already arduous process. By treating the choice as a business decision, you can prioritize objectivity, evaluating candidates based on their track record, competence, and compatibility with your specific needs.

Return on Investment

Every business decision is, at its core, an evaluation of ROI. The expected returns, be it in terms of profit, growth, or any other metric, are weighed against the investment. Similarly, in choosing a divorce attorney, it's prudent to weigh the potential outcomes against the costs involved.

This isn't merely a financial calculation. Investment in a divorce attorney includes not just money but time, emotional energy, and trust. Are you getting the right value for what you're investing in? Does the attorney have a track record of ensuring favorable outcomes for their clients? Are they efficient, minimizing the emotional and temporal duration of the divorce process? These are essential ROI considerations.

Due Diligence is Paramount

Business leaders know that any significant decision demands thorough research and due diligence. Background checks, reference validations, and a deep dive into past performance are standard protocols. In the context of a divorce attorney, similar diligence is imperative.

Seeking references, understanding their reputation in the legal community, and getting a sense of their approach through first consultations can give you a comprehensive picture. Moreover, understanding their experience with cases like yours can offer insights into their potential efficacy as your representative.

Negotiation Skills

In the corporate world, negotiation skills can make or break deals. A savvy businessperson knows the value of having a strong negotiator on their side. Similarly, in the realm of divorce, especially when assets, alimony, and child custody are at stake, negotiation prowess is invaluable.

Your attorney's ability to negotiate can significantly influence the outcome of your divorce, both in terms of tangible assets and broader well-being. By evaluating potential attorneys based on their negotiation skills, much like you would in a business setting, you can position yourself advantageously in the proceedings.

Compatibility and Communication

Every successful business relationship is built on effective communication and compatibility. Mutual understanding, clear exchanges of information, and aligned goals are the hallmarks of prosperous business partnerships. The attorney-client relationship in a divorce scenario is no different.

Beyond their legal acumen, it's essential to assess how well an attorney communicates. Do they offer clarity? Are they receptive to your concerns? Is there a synergy in your communication styles? An attorney might have an impressive track record, but if they don't resonate with your communication needs, the journey can become more challenging. Whay systems does the firm have in place to be sure that you, as the client, never feel like you can't reach them.

Exit Strategy and Future Planning

In business, every venture or partnership is entered into with a clear understanding of exit strategies. These strategies ensure that if things don't pan out as expected, there's a clear, minimally disruptive path out. Similarly, understanding the endgame is crucial in the divorce process.

Your attorney should not just be focused on the immediate proceedings but also on ensuring a future that aligns with your best interests. Whether it's planning for future financial stability, ensuring child custody arrangements are sustainable, or any other long-term considerations, your attorney should have a forward-looking approach.

While the emotional dimensions of divorce are undeniable and valid, there's profound wisdom in approaching some aspects, especially the selection of an attorney, with the strategic clarity of a business decision. It allows for objectivity, ensures the best outcomes, and minimizes the potential pitfalls in an already challenging journey. As with any significant life decision, a balance of heart and head, emotion and strategy, can pave the way for resilience and recovery.

Chapter 6

The Mistakes Most People Make and How to Avoid them

In the realm of divorce proceedings, selecting the right attorney is a decision of paramount importance, yet it is often fraught with some common pitfalls. This chapter aims to shed light on these frequent errors, providing you with the insights needed to avoid them. Our aim is to transform a process that can often seem daunting and fraught with uncertainty into a more structured and informed decision-making journey.

We will explore various misconceptions and oversights that many meet during the attorney selection process. These range from prioritizing superficial criteria, such as the appearance of a law office, to neglecting critical inquiries about an attorney's experience and approach. By identifying these missteps, we intend to offer a path towards a more strategic and result-oriented approach.

Moreover, this chapter is not solely focused on highlighting potential errors; it is also a resource for practical strategies and solutions. Our goal is to provide you with actionable guidance, empowering you to make informed decisions and select a legal representative who aligns with your specific needs and objectives in a divorce proceeding.

As we delve into this chapter, I invite you to engage with the material thoughtfully and critically. The insights provided here are intended to serve as a foundation for making one of the most significant decisions in your divorce journey. I am committed to assisting you in navigating this process with confidence and clarity.

Not Researching the Attorney's Background and Experience

It's essential to ensure that the attorney that you hire specializes in family law or specifically, divorce cases. I am a big fan of looking for the attorney who is focused on one niche of the law. When you do a search, search for "Divorce Attorney." It will return lists of lawyers for you to scroll through; weed out the attorneys who mention every branch of law practice under the sun as what they do. The attorneys who ONLY do divorce are really, really good at divorce because that is all that they do. How much experience do you think that other "do everything" lawyer has with cases like yours?

After your first search and perusal of the results, do thorough research, check their credentials, and read reviews or testimonials from previous clients of at least five attorneys on your short list. There are literally hundreds of thousands of attorneys out here in the world and most of them are not that great, just by the odds. Do yourself a favor and shop from a long list of possible candidates.

When you make your first call ask the intake specialist if there are any current or former clients of the firm that you might speak to in regard to their experience with that firm. If they say yes and provide these, be sure to call the folks and hear what they have to say. That's a big green flag that you are on the right track for hiring a great attorney.

Ignoring Compatibility and Communication Style

Hiring an attorney without considering whether their communication style and personality align with yours can lead to misunderstandings and frustration. Often when new clients come into a divorce attorney's firm they have so much going on with the drama and trauma of the divorce that they can sometimes forget that the attorney is a lawyer and not a therapist. This can lead to hurt feelings and misunderstandings. What you need to know when you are dealing with your attorney is that he/she is committed to guiding you to make the decisions that are in your very best interest and in line with the law. Your ideal attorney is your advocate in front of the court and mediators; you must be comfortable sharing the whole unvarnished truth with your attorney. As we know, the unvarnished truth, in a divorce, can be ugly.

Some firms will offer you a consultation with the attorney you will be working with if you hire them, while most will have you interviewed by an intake specialist who will answer your questions and advise you on the process and cost of your case. The intake team at family law firms generally do a very good job of representing the spirit and essence of the attorney you will be working with, and this type of process is another green flag that you might be interviewing an ideal attorney. An attorney who invests in the care and communication for potential new clients is also very likely to have a high standard of care and communication for people when they become clients.

Some key indications that an attorney is truly invested in their clients' well-being are:

Active Listening: A caring attorney and his team will actively listen to your concerns, questions, and the details of your case without rushing you or dismissing your feelings. They ensure you feel heard and understood.

Clear and Timely Communication: They keep

you informed about the progress of your case and explain complex legal terms and processes in understandable language. In this modern day, an attorney who offers you a secure client portal for communication and conveyance of all of the documents that you will need to share with them during the course of your case is a sign of an attorney who values clear communication. A responsive attorney who replies to your calls, emails, or messages promptly shows that they value your peace of mind.

Personalized Approach: They take the time to understand your specific situation, needs, and goals, rather than applying a one-size-fits-all strategy to your case. This tailored approach shows they are focused on achieving the best possible outcome for you.

Empathy and Support: An attorney and team who show empathy towards your situation and provide support can make the legal process less stressful. They acknowledge the emotional aspects of your case and guide you through it with sensitivity.

Transparency: A caring attorney is transparent about the potential outcomes of your case, their fee structure, and any other costs involved. They set realistic expectations and are honest about the strengths and weaknesses of your case. A caring attorney will walk you through the steps of the case, so that you will never feel like you are "in the dark." There are times during a divorce case when it seems to you like nothing is happening but there are a lot of things working and percolating behind the scenes. It gives you peace of mind as a client to know exactly when those "hurry up and wait" times are in your case.

Availability: They make themselves available to answer your questions and address your concerns, showing that they prioritize your case and value your peace of mind.

Advocacy and Diligence: An attorney who is passionate about advocating for your rights will go the extra mile to ensure your case is thoroughly prepared and presented. Their diligence in researching, filing paperwork promptly, and strategizing reflects their commitment to your cause.

Professionalism with a Personal Touch: While maintaining professionalism, a caring attorney also adds a personal touch by showing genuine interest in your well-being and being considerate of your circumstances. In my opinion, the most caring attorney will always tell you the truth and very often it is not what you think it should be, especially in family law situations. An attorney who will tell you exactly how it is and not sugar-coat the situation into seeming like what you want to believe is a superior attorney. The truth might sting but there is no other choice than to take life on life's terms. The law provides a clear framework for divorce to be executed and it does not deviate.

Chapter 7

Evaluating Cost Vs. Value

Evaluating the cost-to-value of a divorce attorney involves examining various factors that contribute to both the tangible and intangible benefits you receive in relation to the cost. Here are five key considerations:

Experience and Expertise: Assess the firm's experience in handling cases like yours. Experienced attorneys might charge more, but their expertise can lead to a more favorable outcome achieved more quickly, potentially saving you money in the long run. Consider their knowledge in specific areas relevant to your case, such as child custody, asset division, or international divorce laws. Expanding on the importance of assessing a divorce attorney firm's experience and expertise involves considering several key aspects that can significantly impact the outcome of your case and, consequently, the overall value you receive for the fees you pay.

Relevant Experience: Look for a firm specializing in family law, with a strong track record in cases like yours. The nuances of divorce law can vary greatly depending on the specifics of each case, such as high-net-worth divorces, cases involving business ownership, or divorces with complex child custody issues. An attorney with direct experience in these areas will be better equipped to handle your case effectively.

Case Outcomes: Inquire about the outcomes of earlier cases the firm has handled, especially those that closely mirror your own circumstances. While past performance is not always indicative of future results, a history of favorable outcomes in cases similar to yours can be a good indicator of the firm's capability and ability.

Specialized Knowledge: Depending on the complexities of your case, you may need an attorney with expertise in specific areas of divorce law. For example, if your divorce involves cross-border elements, you'll want someone knowledgeable in international divorce laws. If child custody is a central issue, an attorney with a strong background in family court custody battles is essential.

Continuing Education and Certification: The best attorneys stay abreast of the latest developments and changes in family law. Check if the attorneys at the firm pursue continuing education in their field and if they hold any certifications or recognitions from reputable legal organizations. This commitment to staying informed can translate into more effective representation for your case.

Long-Term Financial Implications: Experienced attorneys might command higher fees, but their expertise can lead to faster and more favorable financial settlements, such as better alimony terms, fair asset division, or more suitable child support arrangements. The first higher cost can be offset by the long-term financial benefits secured by a competent attorney.

Strategic Approach: Experienced attorneys are likely to take a strategic approach to your case, using their knowledge to avoid common pitfalls and capitalize on opportunities to strengthen your position. This strategic insight can speed up the process, reduce the number of billable hours, and ultimately lead to a more satisfactory resolution.

When evaluating an attorney's experience and expertise, it's crucial to consider how these factors align with the specific needs and complexities of your case. An attorney's ability to navigate the legal system efficiently, leverage their specialized knowledge, and strategically advocate on your behalf can significantly impact the overall cost-effectiveness and success of your divorce proceedings.

Reputation and Client Reviews: Look at the firm's reputation in the legal community and client testimonials. A firm with a strong reputation might command higher fees, but the value comes from their ability to negotiate effectively, navigate complex legal issues, and potentially secure better settlements or outcomes.

The reputation of a divorce attorney firm within the legal community and the feedback from past clients are crucial indicators of the firm's reliability, professionalism, and effectiveness. These elements can significantly influence your decision-making process when selecting a firm to represent you. Here's a deeper look at the value this reputation offers and the techniques for assessing it:

Trust and Credibility: A firm with a strong reputation is often seen as more trustworthy and credible, not only by potential clients but also by judges, opposing counsel, and other legal professionals. This credibility can enhance the firm's ability to advocate for your interests effectively.

Negotiation Leverage: Attorneys from well-respected firms may possess greater leverage in negotiations due to their proven track record of success and legal acumen. This can lead to more favorable settlement terms, as opposing parties might be more inclined to reach an agreement rather than face a potentially challenging legal battle.

Complex Case Management: Firms that are highly regarded typically have experience handling intricate legal issues and navigating complex cases. This expertise can be invaluable, especially in divorces that involve complicated financial arrangements, international law, or contentious custody disputes.

Outcome Influence: While no attorney can guarantee specific results, those from firms with a strong reputation have a history of securing positive outcomes for their clients. Their strategic approach and deep understanding of the law can significantly impact the final settlement or court ruling.

Techniques for Assessing Reputation and Client Reviews

Online Reviews and Testimonials: Start by searching for reviews on legal directories, the firm's website, and other review platforms. Look for consistent themes in client feedback, paying attention to mentions of the attorneys' professionalism, communication skills, and success rates.

Legal Directories and Rankings: Utilize legal directories that provide rankings and evaluations of attorneys and law firms. These often include peer reviews, which can offer insights into the firm's standing in the legal community.

Referrals and Word-of-Mouth: Personal referrals from friends, family, or professionals can be incredibly valuable. These firsthand accounts can provide a more nuanced view of a firm's capabilities and the client experience.

Bar Association and Professional Groups: Check the local bar association or professional legal organizations for any recognitions, certifications, or memberships the firm or its attorneys have. Active involvement in these groups can be a sign of respect and authority in the legal field.

Case Histories and Public Records: Research

public records of past cases the firm has handled, if available. Success in notable cases or involvement in legal precedents can be a strong indicator of a firm's expertise and reputation.

Consultation Experience: Finally, your personal experience during an initial consultation can provide direct insight into the firm's approach and how they value client relationships. This interaction can be telling of their professionalism and commitment to client satisfaction.

When evaluating a firm's reputation, it's important to consider both the breadth of positive feedback and the quality of the outcomes they've achieved for their clients. A strong reputation built on successful case results and positive client experiences can offer substantial value, potentially leading to more favorable outcomes for your case.

Importance of Communication and Accessibility

Evaluate the firm's responsiveness and willingness to communicate with you. Being able to reach your attorney when you need them is crucial. Firms that provide direct access to your attorney, offer clear communication channels, and respond promptly might offer better value, even if their rates are higher. The number one Bar complaint throughout the United States is lack of communication from attorneys. Ask about how the firm will communicate with you throughout your case.

Effective communication and accessibility are fundamental components of a successful attorney-client relationship, especially in the emotionally charged context of a divorce. The value derived from good communication practices and the accessibility of your attorney can significantly influence both the process and the outcome of your case. Here's an in-depth exploration of why these factors are crucial and what to look for when evaluating a firm's communication and accessibility:

Understanding and Clarity: Divorce proceedings can be complex and stressful. Clear, jargon-free communication from your attorney can help demystify the legal process, making it easier for you to understand your options and the implications of different decisions. This understanding is vital for making informed choices about your case.

Emotional Support and Reassurance: Divorce is not just a legal process but an emotional journey. An attorney who communicates effectively can offer not only legal guidance but also emotional support and reassurance during challenging times. This aspect of the attorney-client relationship can be invaluable.

Real-Time Updates and Strategy Adjustments: The dynamics of a divorce case can change rapidly. Prompt and direct communication from your attorney ensures that you are always up-to-date with the latest developments in your case, allowing for prompt adjustments to your legal strategy if necessary.

Efficiency and Time Management: Efficient communication can hasten the resolution of your case. Delays in communication can lead to missed opportunities or prolonged proceedings, which might increase your legal expenses and extend the emotional toll of the divorce.

Evaluating Communication and Accessibility

Response Time: Assess how quickly the firm or attorney responds to your inquiries. A firm that prioritizes prompt responses, even if just to acknowledge receipt and provide a timeframe for a detailed reply, shows respect for your concerns and a commitment to efficient service.

Communication Channels: Consider the variety of communication channels the firm offers (e.g., phone, email, text, secure client portals) and whether these align with your preferences and needs. Multiple, convenient channels can enhance the ease and effectiveness of your interactions with your attorney.

Direct Access to Your Attorney: Understand the firm's policy on client-attorney interactions. Some firms might filter communication through paralegals or administrative staff, which can be efficient but might also dilute the directness of your contact with your attorney. Firms that ensure you have direct access to your attorney, especially for significant discussions, might offer a higher level of personal service and value.

Clear Communication Style: During your first consultations, pay attention to the attorney's ability to explain legal concepts clearly and to listen actively to your concerns. An attorney who communicates effectively and ensures you feel heard and understood can greatly enhance your comfort and confidence throughout the legal process.

Regular Updates and Check-Ins: Inquire about the firm's policy for updates and case progress reports. Regular, scheduled updates, as well as spontaneous check-ins during critical moments in your case, can keep you well-informed and engaged in the decision-making process.

Cultural and Linguistic Compatibility: If relevant, consider whether the firm can accommodate any cultural sensitivities or language preferences you may have. This compatibility can be particularly important in ensuring clear communication and mutual understanding.

When evaluating a divorce attorney firm, consider how their communication style and accessibility align with your needs and preferences. A firm that excels in these areas can provide a smoother, more supportive experience, potentially reducing the stress of the divorce process and contributing to more favorable outcomes.

Understanding a divorce attorney firm's billing and fee structure is crucial for evaluating the cost-to-value ratio of their services. Transparency in billing practices helps budget for legal expenses and assess the value you're receiving in exchange for the fees paid. Here's an expanded look at various aspects of billing and fee structures and why they're important:

Components of Billing and Fee Structures

Hourly Rates: Many divorce attorneys charge by the hour, with rates varying based on experience, reputation, and geographic location. Understanding the hourly rate is straightforward, but it's important to get an estimate of how many hours your case might take, recognizing that unpredictable complexities can arise.

Flat Fees: Some firms offer flat-fee arrangements for more straightforward cases, covering all legal services under a single, fixed price. This can be cost-effective and provides certainty about legal expenses, but make sure you understand what is and isn't included to avoid unexpected charges.

Retainer Fees: A retainer is an upfront fee paid to secure the attorney's services, often used against hourly billing as your case progresses. Understanding how the retainer is applied, what happens when it's depleted, and whether any unused portion is refundable is key to managing your finances.

Additional Costs: Be aware of potential additional costs that might not be included in the attorney's fees, such as court filing fees, costs for expert witnesses or consultants, and charges for administrative tasks performed by support staff. These can add up and should be factored into your overall budget.

Contingency Fees: While less common in divorce cases, some aspects, like spousal support or child support recovery, might be handled on a contingency basis, where the attorney's fee is a percentage of the amount recovered. Ensure you understand the percentage and how it's calculated.

Importance of Transparency and Fairness

No Hidden Costs: A firm that provides a detailed

breakdown of its fee structure, including what each charge covers, is likely to be more trustworthy and fair. This transparency helps prevent surprises and allows for better financial planning.

Value Assessment: By understanding the fee structure, you can better assess the value you're receiving. For example, a higher hourly rate might be justified by the attorney's level of experience, specialization, or efficiency in handling cases like yours.

Negotiation and Customization: Some firms might be willing to negotiate their fees or offer customized billing arrangements to fit your financial situation. This flexibility can be particularly valuable in complex cases that might require extensive legal work.

Evaluating Billing Arrangements for Your Situation

Assessment of Needs: Evaluate the complexity of

your case and your specific needs to decide which billing structure might be most cost-effective for you. For instance, a flat fee might be more suitable for a straightforward case without contested elements, while an hourly rate could be more appropriate for a complex case requiring extensive negotiation or litigation.

Communication of Budget Constraints: Be upfront about your budget constraints with potential attorneys. A firm that's willing to discuss and accommodate your financial situation, possibly through a customized billing arrangement, can provide greater value.

Comparison and Negotiation: Don't hesitate to compare fee structures from different firms and negotiate terms. Understanding the market rate for similar services in your area can provide leverage in these discussions.

In sum, a clear and fair billing and fee structure is

foundational to setting up a trust-based relationship with your divorce attorney. It enables you to make informed decisions about your legal representation, manage your finances effectively, and ultimately find the best attorney to meet your needs and circumstances.

Understanding Personal Fit

The aspect of personal fit and support in the context of a divorce attorney firm extends beyond the mere provision of legal services. It encompasses the emotional, psychological, and sometimes even practical support that a client receives during the divorce process. Given the inherently personal and often emotionally charged nature of divorce, the level of support and attention provided by your attorney can significantly impact your experience and the overall outcome of your case. Here is a deeper exploration of why personal fit and support are so crucial:

Empathy and Understanding: An attorney who demonstrates empathy and takes the time to understand not just the legal, but also the emotional and personal aspects of your case, can provide more compassionate and effective representation. This understanding can inform their approach, ensuring it aligns with your specific needs and concerns.

Communication Style: The way an attorney communicates can affect your comfort level and confidence in their representation. An attorney whose communication style matches your own, who listens actively, and explains legal concepts in a way that you understand, can make the process less daunting and more collaborative.

Availability and Accessibility: Feeling that your attorney is there for you, ready to address your concerns and answer your questions, can provide significant peace of mind. An attorney who makes themselves available, promptly returns calls or emails, and takes the time to check in on you can make a substantial difference in your experience.

Importance of Support and Guidance

Navigating Emotional Waters: Divorce can be

one of the most stressful life events. An attorney who provides legal guidance and emotional support can help you navigate this challenging time more effectively, helping you make decisions not clouded by emotion.

Strategic Decision-Making: An attorney who understands your personal goals and concerns can provide tailored advice that considers both the legal and emotional outcomes of various decisions. This level of personalized strategy can lead to more satisfactory results in both the short and long term.

Holistic Approach: Some firms may offer or recommend support services beyond legal advice, such as counseling or mediation, to help manage the emotional aspects of divorce. This comprehensive approach can contribute to a more positive and constructive divorce process.

Evaluating Personal Fit and Support

Initial Consultations: Use initial consultations

not just to discuss your case, but to gauge the attorney's empathy, listening skills, and overall demeanor. You should feel heard, respected, and comfortable during these interactions.

Client Testimonials: Look for reviews or testimonials from past clients that specifically mention the level of support and personal attention they received. These can provide insights into the attorney's approach to client relationships.

Questions to Ask: Consider asking potential attorneys about their approach to client support, how they handle the emotional aspects of divorce cases, and what you can expect in terms of communication and availability.

Trust Your Instincts: Your gut feeling after meeting with an attorney can be a powerful indicator of personal fit. You should feel confident in their capabilities and comfortable with their approach to your case.

While the cost of legal services is an important consideration, the value of a strong personal fit and comprehensive support during a divorce cannot be overstated. An attorney who provides tailored advice, emotional support, and a high level of personal attention can make the divorce process more bearable and can help you achieve outcomes that align with your overall well-being and future goals.

Chapter 8

Decide, Hire & Step into Your New Life!

Choosing the ideal divorce attorney after interviewing several candidates involves a thoughtful analysis of each attorney's qualifications, your comfort level with them, and how well they align with your specific needs and goals. Here are some key factors to consider when making your decision:

Experience and Specialization: Evaluate each attorney's experience not just in family law but in cases similar to yours. Specialization in divorce cases, especially those with complexities like yours (such as child custody, high-net-worth divorces, etc.), can be an advantage.

Communication and Compatibility: Consider how well you communicate with the attorney and whether you feel understood and respected. It's crucial that you're comfortable sharing personal details with them and that they show empathy and a clear understanding of your situation.

Strategy and Approach: Reflect on the strategy each attorney proposes for your case. Do they suggest an aggressive approach when you prefer mediation? Ensure their approach aligns with your values and goals for the divorce outcome.

Availability and Responsiveness: Assess each attorney's availability to take on your case and their responsiveness to your communications. You need someone who will be accessible and prompt in updating you about your case progress.

References and Reputation: Consider feedback from past clients if available. An attorney's reputation among clients and in the legal community can offer insights into their professionalism and effectiveness.

Fee Structure and Affordability: Understand each attorney's fee structure and ensure it is transparent and reasonable. While cost shouldn't be the sole deciding factor, it's important to choose an attorney whose services you can afford without compromising quality.

Personal Comfort and Trust: Ultimately, your gut feeling about the attorney's trustworthiness and your personal comfort level with them can be a deciding factor. You should feel confident in their abilities and comfortable with their guidance.

Case Management and Team: Inquire about who will be handling your case. Some attorneys work with a team, while others handle everything personally. Ensure you're comfortable with the arrangement and that you know who your points of contact will be.

Outcome Expectations: Consider how realistic and transparent each attorney is about the potential outcomes of your case. It's important that they set realistic expectations and are not just telling you what they think you want to hear.

Compatibility with Your Goals: Ensure the attorney's approach and philosophy about divorce align with your own. For instance, if you're aiming for a collaborative divorce, an attorney known for their contentious approach might not be the best fit.

After considering these factors, narrow down your choices to the attorney who best meets your needs and with whom you feel most comfortable. It's also helpful to take some time to reflect on your discussions and feelings after the interviews before making a final decision.

Once you've chosen an attorney to represent you in your divorce, approaching them to formalize your working relationship and understanding the common next steps in the divorce process are crucial. Here's a guide on how to proceed:

Approaching the Chosen Attorney

Confirmation: Contact the attorney to confirm your decision to hire them. This can be done via phone, email, or a follow-up meeting, depending on your prior communications.

Retainer Agreement: The attorney will likely provide a retainer agreement or contract for you to review and sign. This document outlines the scope of their services, fee structure, and other terms of your engagement.

Retainer Fee: Most divorce attorneys require a retainer fee upfront. This is a pre-payment for their services that will be held in trust and billed against for hours worked and expenses incurred. Some attorneys will offer you a more transparent and straightforward Flat Fee Billing, which will be detailed in your Agreement Letter.

Documentation: Provide any documentation or information the attorney has requested. This may include financial records, marriage certificates, prenuptial agreements, details about assets and liabilities, and any other relevant information to your case. In some instances, the firm will have a form or two to guide you along providing all the pertinent information.

Initial Meeting: Arrange a first meeting or a follow-up meeting to discuss the specifics of your case, your goals, and any immediate concerns or questions you have. This is an opportunity to establish a communication plan and discuss how often and through what means you will receive updates. Be prepared to meet the Team and learn the firm's procedures so that you can help to expedite your case.

Now that you have decided who to hire and understand those next steps, I would like to give you a brief overview of the flow of a common divorce case.

Common Next Steps in a Divorce

Filing the Petition: Your attorney will prepare and file a petition for divorce with the appropriate court. This document formally starts the divorce process and outlines your initial legal positions and desired outcomes.

Serving the Petition: The petition must be legally

served to your spouse, notifying them of the divorce proceedings. Your spouse will have a specified period to respond.

Temporary Orders: If necessary, your attorney may file for temporary court orders to address immediate needs such as child custody, support, and property issues while the divorce is pending.

Discovery Process: Both parties exchange information and documents related to finances, assets, debts, and other relevant matters. This may involve written questions (interrogatories), document requests, and depositions.

Negotiation and Mediation: Many divorce cases are resolved through negotiation or mediation, where both parties, often with the help of their attorneys and possibly a mediator, work out a settlement agreement on various issues like property division, child custody, and support.

Trial: If a settlement cannot be reached, the case may go to trial, where a judge will make decisions on all contested issues. Trials can be lengthy and expensive, so they are generally considered a last resort.

Final Judgment: Once an agreement is reached or a trial concludes, the court will issue a final divorce decree, legally ending the marriage and outlining the terms of the divorce, including asset division, custody arrangements, support, and any other relevant details.

Post-Divorce Actions: After the divorce is finalized, there may be steps to implement the court's orders, such as transferring property titles, adjusting insurance policies, and updating estate plans.

Throughout this process, your attorney will guide you, represent your interests, and keep you informed about the progress of your case. It's essential to maintain open communication with your attorney and to promptly provide any requested information or documentation to help your case proceed smoothly.

Embarking on a new life after divorce can be a

significant transition, marked by both challenges and opportunities for personal growth and new beginnings. Here are some suggestions on how to approach your new life post-divorce:

Embrace the Change

Acceptance: Acknowledge the change in your marital status and embrace it as a new chapter in your life. It's okay to grieve the loss, but also important to accept it and move forward. Do not isolate yourself! That is deeply unhealthy and if you feel the urge to do this I highly recommend that you find a therapist or divorce support group to speak with.

Positive Outlook: Try to maintain a positive outlook on your future. View this as an opportunity to rediscover yourself, your interests, and your aspirations. You are not starting over with nothing; you are beginning with experience!

Focus on Self-Care

Physical Health: Maintain a healthy lifestyle

through regular exercise, a balanced diet, and sufficient sleep. Physical well-being significantly impacts mental health. We are so blessed to live in a wonderful golden age where inspiration and education are just a quick search on YouTube away! Do not neglect the resources that we sometimes overlook!

Mental Health: Allow yourself time to heal emotionally. Consider seeking support from a therapist or counselor to navigate your feelings and adjust to your new life. Divorce support groups or grief/loss counseling can be tremendously helpful as you make the transition from married to single.

Social Support: Lean on friends and family for support. Consider joining support groups or communities where you can meet others who are going through similar experiences.

Rediscover Yourself

New Interests: Explore new hobbies, interests, or activities that you may not have had time for in the past. This can be a great way to meet new people and expand your social circle.

Personal Goals: Set new personal and professional goals. This might include career advancement, education, travel, or any other aspirations you've put on hold.

Financial Independence

Budgeting: Establish a new budget that reflects your current income and expenses as a single person. This might involve adjusting to a different lifestyle or financial priorities. I personally love and highly recommend the budgeting software: You Need A Budget. There is a book by the same name that is fantastic. It puts a little different spin on a dry and yucky topic and almost gamifies your finances. It's really fun! Check it out, www.ynab.com

Financial Planning: Consider consulting with a financial advisor to plan for your future, including savings, investments, retirement, and any other financial goals you have.

Parenting Adjustments

If you have children, focus on maintaining a stable and positive environment for them. Open communication and a cooperative co-parenting arrangement with your ex-spouse can help ease the transition for your children. Parenting apps can be especially helpful if you don't have great communication with the other parent.

Build a Supportive Network

New Relationships: Gradually build new relationships, both friendships and romantic, when you feel ready. Take things slowly and focus on building meaningful connections. Remember that we tend to become like those we spend time with so choose who you are spending your time with wisely. Hanging out with a bunch of bitter people will not improve your life or situation.

Community Engagement: Engage with your community through volunteering, clubs, or local events. This can provide a sense of belonging and purpose.

Personal Reflection and Growth

Reflection: Spend time reflecting on your past relationship to understand what you can learn from it. This can be crucial for personal growth and in forming healthier relationships in the future.

Self-Development: Invest in self-improvement through courses, workshops, or reading. Continuous learning and development can boost your confidence and sense of self-worth.

Take Your Time

Remember, there's no rush to figure everything out immediately. Allow yourself the time to adjust and explore this new phase of your life at your own pace.

Approaching life after divorce with a mindset geared towards personal growth, healing, and exploration can transform this period into a profoundly enriching experience. Each step you take towards rebuilding can lead to newfound strengths and opportunities.

When you are ready to launch successfully into your next big step consider the support of a performance coach to help you achieve your goals with ease and speed! Do not go it alone, doing it the hard way, if you do not have to! I offer performance coaching for select clients. You can find out more at www.theladystoic.com

ABOUT THE AUTHOR

Nichole Wilde Hart knows all about divorce, from the inside and the outside. Divorced twice herself and the operator of a successful client services firm for premier divorce attorneys throughout the United States, she has an intimate understanding of the concerns people are trying to alleviate when they are seeking the professional help of an attorney for a divorce. If you are shopping for an attorney the odds are, you are in a stressful situation. Nichole wrote this book to help you understand why and how hiring the ideal professional can be of value to you, help relieve some of your stress, help you streamline the process of choosing your attorney so that you can clean up that old relationship and move on with your life as soon as possible. She lives joyfully with her husband, where they split their time near Seattle, Washington and Birmingham, Alabama. She offers performance coaching for select clients (www.theladystoic.com) and enjoys quilting, hiking, weightlifting and travel.

Ideal Attorney Checklist:

Use this Checklist for your attorney interviews.

Firm:

Phone:

How will you keep me informed about my case?

What details of my case give you pause for concern? Why? How will you address them?

How does your firm handle communication? What can I expect for a response time from my legal team if I hire you?

How does the average case like mine proceed? What can I expect?

Ideal Attorney Checklist:

Use this Checklist for your attorney interviews.

Firm:

Phone:

How will you keep me informed about my case?

What details of my case give you pause for concern? Why? How will you address them?

How does your firm handle communication? What can I expect for a response time from my legal team if I hire you?

How does the average case like mine proceed? What can I expect?

Notes

Ideal Attorney Checklist:

Use this Checklist for your attorney interviews.

Firm:

Phone:

How will you keep me informed about my case?

What details of my case give you pause for concern? Why? How will you address them?

How does your firm handle communication? What can I expect for a response time from my legal team if I hire you?

How does the average case like mine proceed? What can I expect?